Our Lady gives

the

Rosary of the *Unborn*™

to conquer abortion

Second Edition

"Solemnly I tell you, recognize abortion as a face of evil and an enemy to world security. You will not have genuine peace until abortion is overturned."
Jesus October 5, 2001

"Spread devotion to the Rosary of the Unborn like the enemy would spread germ warfare. Let this devotion permeate cities, nations and the heart of the world. When you pray this special prayer, you combat war in the womb and war in the world."
Jesus March 5, 2003

Archangel Gabriel Enterprises Inc.

ABOUT THE APPARITIONS

Since 1985, Jesus and Blessed Mother have been appearing to Maureen Sweeney-Kyle on an almost daily basis and have given her a series of missions to accomplish.

1986 – 1990
*OUR LADY PROTECTRESS OF THE FAITH

1990 – 1993
PROJECT MERCY
(NATIONWIDE ANTI-ABORTION ROSARY CRUSADES)

1993 – Present
The combined revelations of **MARY, REFUGE OF HOLY LOVE** and the **CHAMBERS OF THE UNITED HEARTS**. In 1993 Our Lady asked that this mission be known as **HOLY LOVE MINISTRIES**.

*On August 28, 1988, Our Lady came as "Guardian of the Faith" to Visionary Patricia Talbot of Cuenca, Ecuador, in South America. In 1991, the Bishops of Ibarra and Guayaquil in Ecuador approved the movement which contains the name "Guardian of the Faith" and thus implicitly the title.

Visionary:
Maureen is a very shy, timid and frail housewife and grandmother. She grew up and still resides in the Cleveland, Ohio area with her husband.

In 1993, Our Lady began **Holy Love Ministries** and then requested that the ministry procure property for a shrine in Lorain County, Ohio. This was accomplished in 1995 (115 acres) and is now known as **Maranatha Spring & Shrine**, home of **Holy Love Ministries**, an Ecumenical Lay Apostolate to make known to the world the Chambers of the United Hearts.

Spiritual Director:
   Over the past twenty years, Maureen has had four spiritual directors who have been experts in Marian Theology.

On the joyful occasion of the visit by the visionary, Maureen Sweeney-Kyle, with Pope John Paul II in August of 1999. Her husband, Don (lower right), the Late Archbishop Gabriel Ganaka (top left), and Rev. Frank Kenney, her Spiritual Director (1994-2004) (top center), accompanied her on the visit.

HOW DID THIS UNIQUE ROSARY COME ABOUT AND THE PROMISES ATTENDANT TO IT?

On October 7, 1997– the Feast of the Holy Rosary – Our Lady appeared to visionary Maureen Sweeney-Kyle with this rosary and stated:

…"Propagate the image I have shown you today."

October 7, 1997 – *Feast of the Holy Rosary*

Our Lady comes in white. In front of Her and suspended in the air is an unusual rosary. The Our Father beads are droplets of blood in the shape of a cross. The Hail Mary beads are light blue tear drops with unborn babies inside of them. The cross is gleaming gold. Our Lady says: "I come in praise of Jesus, My Son. I come as Prophetess of these times."

"The rosary you see is Heaven's way of describing to you the weapon that will overcome this evil of abortion. Heaven weeps for the cost of this great sin. The history and the future of all nations has been changed because of this atrocity against God's gift of life."

"Today, sadly, much responsibility must be placed on the laity who are consecrated to Me. I cannot depend on Church leadership to unite in an effort to vanquish the enemy through the Rosary. Even My apparitions have caused division by Satan's efforts to thwart My plans."

"So today, on My feast day, I am calling all My children to unite in My Heart. Do not allow pride to divide you according to which apparition you will follow. Become part of the Flame of My Heart. Be united in love and in the prayer weapon of My Rosary. The evil of abortion can be conquered by your efforts and through My grace."

"Propagate the image I have shown you today."

<u>Heaven's Promises</u>

When this handmade rosary was finally completed and ready for distribution 3 1/2 years later, Our Lady and Jesus gave Maureen the following promises regarding this unique rosary:

July 2, 2001 Afternoon

Our Lady comes as the Sorrowful Mother. She says: "Praise be to Jesus. I see you are using the new Rosary of the Unborn. **I affirm to you, my daughter, that each 'Hail Mary' prayed from a loving heart will rescue one of these innocent lives from death by abortion. When you use this rosary, call to mind My Sorrowful Immaculate Heart which continually sees the sin of abortion played out in every present moment.** I give to you this special sacramental* with which to heal My Motherly Heart."

Maureen asks: "Blessed Mother, do you mean any 'Hail Mary' or just one prayed on the Rosary of the Unborn?"

Blessed Mother: "This is a special grace attached to this particular rosary. It should always be used to pray against abortion. You will please make this known."

*Note: In order to be a sacramental, it must be blessed by a Catholic Priest.

July 2, 2001 Evening

Blessed Mother is here as Mary, Refuge of Holy Love. She is holding the Rosary of the Unborn and says: "Praise be to Jesus."

"You can be confident in using this rosary and the attached attendant promise I have given you. Do not be abashed (shy) about propagating this message."

August 3, 2001

"I am your Jesus, born Incarnate. Trust in Me. Please tell the world that each 'Our Father' (beads shown to Maureen by Jesus were teardrops of blood in the form of a cross) recited on the Rosary of the Unborn assuages My grieving Heart. Further, it withholds the Arm of Justice."

"The greatest promise I give you in regards to this rosary is this: Every Rosary prayed from the heart to its completion on these beads mitigates the punishment as yet withstanding for the sin of abortion."

Later that day:

I told Jesus I had a question about the promise He gave concerning the Rosary of the Unborn. He finally returned, all aglow. He smiled and said:

"I am your Jesus, born Incarnate. I know your question. Do not bother to speak it. **When I say the punishment as yet withstanding for the sin of abortion, I mean the punishment each soul deserves for taking part in this sin. Then too, I also refer to the greater punishment that awaits the world for embracing this sin."**

"Pray from your heart knowing that your Rosary appeases Me."

May 29, 2002

"I am your Jesus, born Incarnate. I have come to speak publicly about the Rosary of the Unborn. This is a great gift given from Heaven in and through this Mission of Holy Love. My Mother has designed this rosary Herself, and with Her approval it is now being reproduced. Many and important promises are attendant to this unique rosary of Her design."

"In the world there are those who have set about to counterfeit this special rosary. I am asking the faithful— do not be fooled. It is the rosary given here at this mission of Holy Love that carries with it the promises from Heaven."

"Make it known."

February 28, 2005

"I am your Jesus, born Incarnate."

"What My Mother told you last night concerning the Rosary of the Unborn is this. If a group is gathered who are praying for the unborn from the heart and only one person has in their possession the Rosary of the Unborn, I will honor each 'Hail Mary' from each person in the group as if they were holding the Rosary of the Unborn themselves."

"In this way I lift the constraint of time which it takes to produce enough rosaries."

Maureen says: "Thank you, Jesus."

Heaven's Victory

February 2, 2002

"Praise be to Jesus. My daughter, it is with docility I come to tell you that Jesus is passing on to the world through My Maternal Heart this Rosary of the Unborn. Never before in the history of mankind has motherhood been so maligned and misrepresented. Never before has the life of the unborn been in such jeopardy. But through faithful recitation of the rosary on these beads I have presented to you, Satan's plans will be thwarted and natural motherhood raised once again to its place of distinction."

"Jesus has chosen this century through the Will of His Father for a return to the reality of life within the womb which will be a stepping stone to His victory."

Blessed Mother

March 18, 2002

Our Lady comes as Refuge of Holy Love with many angels. They are bowing to Her. She says: "Praise be to Jesus."

"I have come to show you this." She shows me the Rosary of the Unborn wrapped around a beautiful gold crown."

"This is My Crown of Victory. **See and understand that this Rosary of the Unborn is an integral part of My Victory, both in hearts and in the world.**"

"Jesus desires that you make this known."

MESSAGES ABOUT ABORTION

October 14, 2001
Second Sunday Service to Pray against Abortion

Jesus is here with His Heart exposed. He says: "I am your Jesus, born Incarnate."

"I am Sovereign Good which must reign in every heart. Once again I come to tell you that **if your nation overturns legalized abortion, I will richly bless it by my favor. But if this sin continues with national approval, much will be stripped away.** My brothers and sisters, recognize **evil** and pray against it."

"I'm blessing you with My Blessing of Divine Love."

*THREE DAYS AFTER
THE 9/11 TERRORIST ATTACK
IN NEW YORK*

September 15, 2001 Midnight Rosary
At the Sorrowful Mother Shrine/Lake of Tears
Feasts of The Exaltation of the Cross
and Our Lady of Sorrows

Blessed Mother is here as Our Lady of Sorrows. She says: "Praise be to Jesus."

"Dear children, during this hour of grief, understand that your Heavenly Mother stands at the foot of the Cross with you. I sorrow with you for this senseless loss of life. Place your sorrow deep within the wounds of My Jesus."

"My message to you as a nation is this: **GOD alone is the giver and taker of life.** Whenever man presumes to take upon himself the role of God, the world is changed forever."

"**A stark parallel emerges from this national tragedy. Within minutes the false sense of security this nation enjoyed was stripped away. Lives were destroyed. Violent death was incurred upon the innocent. So too, in the womb the security of the innocent baby is destroyed within minutes. Life is destroyed by the evil plans of another. It is called 'abortion', but it varies little from the national disaster your nation now mourns. Yet, who mourns with Me at the foot of the Cross for the senseless loss of these innocent lives? As a nation I invite you – I plead with you – to do so. Do not mourn one national tragedy and ignore the other.**"

"**Just as the planes became instruments of death by penetrating those buildings with a destructive force, so too, the instruments of the abortionists invade the privacy of the womb – wielding death. In each case the terrorists and the participants in abortion feel justified through convoluted thinking.**"

"But My Son, the Just Judge, does not reason this way. He reasons with a righteous Heart. In His Infinite Mercy He stands ready to forgive the contrite heart – even the heart guilty of such heinous acts as these. My Jesus does not forgive the unrepentant."

"My dear children, I have come to you so that you may be reconciled with God. The path of reconciliation is Holy

Love. The path of judgment is arrogance, hatred and vengeance. God's judgment falls upon those people and nations who do not live in love. Therefore, I have come to call all people and every nation under the seal of Holy Love."

"If you live in Holy Love – that is, your heart is loving – you will have love in your world around you. If you have evil in your heart, that too, will spread to the world around you. Evil begets evil. Love begets love."

"My dear, dear little children, tonight more than ever, I need you to abandon yourselves to my Immaculate Heart which is Holy Love. When you begin to live these messages and hold them in your heart, you come under the seal of Holy Love. This is a special sign of your predestination, your salvation, and it is a sign to Satan that you belong to me. You do not have to travel many miles over land and sea to receive this special seal. For this seal is yours when you begin to live these messages."

"Tonight my dear, dear children, my sympathy rests upon you. My prayers are with you, and I am carrying your petitions to Heaven. Do not fear – I am holding you in my arms, and tonight I am blessing you with My Blessing of Holy Love."

WHY DID 9/11 OCCUR?
GOD'S PERMITTING WILL

October 20, 2001

St. Thomas Aquinas comes. He says: "Today I come in praise of Jesus, Lord and Savior. I come to explain to you God's Permitting Will. Think of God's Divine Will as a great umbrella protecting the earth. God's Will protects from all evil **(God's Ordaining Will)**. But God does not interfere with the free will of man. Now, when man chooses to oppose God's Will and sins, it is as though a hole is made in the umbrella. Then the protection of the Father's Will is not complete as He planned it to be. This 'hole' allows or permits Satan to come in and execute his plans. So you see, God's Permitting Will is not what He chooses for humanity, but what man chooses and God allows."

"It causes the Eternal Father great pain to see what man opens himself up to through sin. Our Heavenly Mother weeps. Oh, how She weeps to see the destruction brought about by sin. You should make this known."

July 7, 2001

"I am your Jesus, born Incarnate. I have come today to help all people understand that the laws which govern against the Law of Love are the fruits of convoluted consciences. I look into the heart and judge according to what is in each heart."

"It is pride that leads the soul off track. It is pride that works against truth. I watch in sorrow the sins against the innocents from My Throne in Heaven. Such error does not exist in a humble soul, but only in the proud of heart."

"My Mother has prescribed for you the Rosary of the Unborn to overcome this great error and grave sin. I never tire of hearing it. It is balm to My wounded Heart."

October 6, 2001

Jesus is here with His Heart exposed. He says: "I am your Jesus, born Incarnate."

"My brothers and sisters, every prayer you say against abortion defeats Satan in someone's life, in some way. Come against this heinous crime, the killing of the unborn. Every prayer you say repairs My Heart which is in anguish over this sin."

"Tonight I'm blessing you with My Blessing of Divine Love."

October 12, 2001

"I am your Jesus, born Incarnate. My messenger, please understand that **the more man tries to become like God, the more he will be humbled. The more humanity assumes the role of giver and taker of life, the more self-centeredness and hatred will flourish in hearts.**"

"Once again I remind mankind that what lies in the center of his heart monopolizes his thoughts, words and actions, for it is the heart that governs free will. This is why My Mother and I urge and direct humanity to allow Holy Love possession of your heart."

"The prince of lies tries to dissuade each one from this course. If you realize this, it should not be difficult to discover his suggestions. Do not allow him any doorway of opportunity."

"Be mindful of these, My words to you today, and make them known."

October 5, 2001 – Monthly Message to All Nations

Jesus and Blessed Mother are here with Their Hearts exposed. Blessed Mother says: "Praise be to Jesus." (Jesus and Blessed Mother were surrounded by the Rosary of the Unborn. There were large angels stationed at each of the 'Our Father' beads.)

Jesus: "I am your Jesus, born Incarnate. **I have come to ask you to stop killing the life I lovingly place in the womb. Each life that is snuffed out changes the world forever.**"

"My brothers and sisters, I come to you today clothed in truth and openness. I hide nothing from you. **I have no ulterior motive aside from the safety, salvation and well-being of every soul from the moment of conception until natural death. I beg your country today to take heed of My call to end legalized abortion.** Do not wait until My solution is your last alternative."

"I desire that all humanity unite under the Seal of Holy and Divine Love—the two great commandments that embrace all the commandments. Yes, I long to place My Kiss of Divine Love upon the heart of the world. Then abortion would cease—war would end and terror would lose her grip upon the throat of the world."

"My brothers and sisters, it is when you do not place God first, and when you do not love your neighbor as you do yourselves, that right reason leaves you. Your consciences become compromised and you cannot distinguish good from evil. This is the state of confusion governments are in when they legislate unjust laws. It is the state of convoluted thinking that leads people to acts of terror. This is how souls open their hearts to Satan. The world cannot prosper in such confusion. Little by little, Satan is establishing his anarchy—first in hearts—then in the world."

"**But I have come to tell you what the adversary does not want you to hear; that is, that every Mass you attend, every Communion you receive, every Holy Hour you make, every prayer or rosary you say, weakens the enemy forever in some soul somewhere in the world**. This is the way to victory, little by little—one soul at a time patiently persevering in Holy Love."

"The war you are engaged in is not over property or even lives. It is about souls. It is good against evil. This is why I come here today seeking to place My Seal upon your hearts. My Seal is Holy and Divine Love. It is a sign to Satan that you belong to Me spiritually, and he can't have you. But I can only place My Seal upon your heart when you obey the two great commandments of love. Hasten to live the message and begin your journey through the Chambers of Our United Hearts; for when I return in Victory, all will be in the Fifth Chamber of My Heart—the Kingdom of the Divine Will."

"**In truth I tell you that your nation's stance on legalized abortion is the determining factor in your national security.** For years Heaven has stood by and watched as the security of the baby in the womb was violated and life taken. Solemnly I tell you, recognize abortion as a face of evil and an enemy to world security. **You will not have genuine peace until abortion is**

overturned. Do not see My words to you today as a threat, but as a grace."

"We are blessing you with the Blessing of Our United Hearts."

September 10, 2006
Second Sunday Service to Pray against Abortion

Jesus is here with His Heart exposed. He says: "I am your Jesus, born Incarnate."

"My brothers and sisters, tomorrow your country will commemorate the loss of life during the September 11th tragedy five years ago. Certainly this is a great loss, but who mourns for the loss of life sacrificed on the altar of abortion, moment by moment, day to day? Who sorrows for the loss of innocence at an early age, which is becoming commonplace around the world?"

"Until all life is respected from conception until natural death, you will continue to have violence, terrorism and wars at your doorstep. Therefore, if you want violence and terrorism to end, then you must pray for all of life to be respected."

"I'm blessing you with My Blessing of Divine Love."

MESSAGES ABOUT PRAYER

April 24, 1999

"I have come to you today as your Jesus, born Incarnate. I wish today to teach you about prayer. Prayer is a refuge or weapon and a means of unification – creature to Creator. The more the soul surrenders his own will to the Will of God, the deeper his union through prayer."

"Surrender then your plans, your choices, your desires. No good comes to you except through God. In this surrender you are engaging all the virtues – faith, hope, love, humility, simplicity, meekness, trust."

"Prayer is communication with God, either in the heart, on the lips, or through any action that is surrendered to the Divine Will."

"My Mother prays with you when you pray the Rosary. Her Heart is a channel through which your prayers ascend to Heaven and grace passes back down to you. Her Heart is a connection then to God and God's grace, just as you would connect an electric light to currents."

"God receives the sacrifice of prayer and uses it as a sword against evil. He changes the prayer into grace that overcomes evil in hearts. Then see, it is Satan that tries to keep you from praying. It is Satan who embattles your heart and tries to keep you from surrendering your will so that you can pray."

"No matter your course of action in any event, everything depends on God. Trust this. The soul that trusts only in himself is lost."

"Think of prayer as a sunbeam. Its ray stretches down from Heaven. It nourishes the lilies and flowers. It royally clothes them in light. Thus arrayed, they bloom and their beauty gives glory to God. The soul that surrenders to prayer much, also becomes beautiful in God's eyes and gives glory to God."

"I have told you, My confidante, that prayer is a surrender and a sacrifice. But the soul must also accept the way prayers are answered. The little flower receives what it needs to be nourished and grow. The soul, through prayer, receives what it needs for salvation. In humility, he must accept God's Will. If the Father knows what the little flower needs, does he not know your needs as well? Accept what He sends you in humility and gratefulness, like the little flower dancing in the sunlight."

"I am pleased with any prayer. Most of all I am pleased with sincere prayer from the heart. This kind of prayer changes people and events. I, your Jesus, love the prayer of the Mass the most. Then I love the Rosary."

"Follow Me in prayer. I will lead you."

September 18, 1999

"I have come to speak to you about prayer, and in particular the prayer of the Rosary. I am your Jesus, born Incarnate. So many surrender to prayer without the sentiment of love in their hearts. This weakens the prayer, making it less worthy. Instead, bolster your prayers by recalling the love you have in your heart for Me and My Mother. This allows Me to pour the choicest graces upon you and into your life."

"Prayer has a cumulative effect. I know ahead of time how many prayers will be offered for each petition. Therefore, you never know what just one more Hail Mary will bring. One Hail Mary said with a loving heart has the power to stop wars, bring nature into harmony with God's plan, convert an unbeliever, save a vocation, deliver a soul from purgatory, and change the future forever. Think, then, of the power of a whole Rosary said with love."

"Satan knows that the Rosary is the weapon which will bring about his defeat. This is why he is desperate to discourage its use. Every time you recite a Hail Mary from the heart, the devil is weakened forever in some area and in some soul."

"You must never be discouraged, then, in praying the Rosary. When your heart is most filled with distraction, understand the adversary is frightened of your prayers."

"The Heart of My Mother is consoled by your efforts in prayer. She is most indebted to the ones who persevered in a regimen of prayer despite opposition."

"Make it known."

September 28, 1998

Our Lady comes in bluish gray and white. She is holding a big mixing bowl.

She says: "Praise, honor, and glory to Jesus. My daughter, perhaps this is a bit simplistic, but I wish to compare prayer to the baking of a cake – a task I have watched you perform often."

"The bowl is Holy Love, for without the bowl nothing

comes together to form the final product (the cake). The batter is the words of the prayer. It has many ingredients (many words that make up the whole). The batter is placed in a pan. The pan represents prayer intentions such as, petition, thanksgiving, praise, etc. The cake is baked in an oven, which represents the action of the Holy Spirit in the heart as you pray. The final product, the cake, is the prayer the angels take into Heaven for you. While this process of prayer is going on, there are many, many ways the universe is affected. Satan sends his cohorts to attack the person at prayer. (He wants to make the cake fall, the prayer less effective.) The good angels are waging war with the evil spirits trying to allow the prayer to rise to Heaven. Meanwhile, in Heaven, the frosting, or grace, is being prepared for every prayer being offered. Even a cupcake is frosted. Therefore, see even the smallest ejaculatory prayer merits grace."

"I am always with you when you pray. I measure your breath, watch your lips as they pronounce each word, and call you into the presence of God. It is so with each soul. If you forget an ingredient, I add it. I love to flavor your prayers with My love. Therefore, see that you cannot fail in this endeavor, for I am blessing you, I am baking the cake with you."

She smiles and leaves.

April 5, 2002 – Monthly Message to All Nations

Jesus and Blessed Mother are here with Their Hearts exposed. Blessed Mother says: "Praise be to Jesus." Jesus and Our Lady greet Father Kenney (Maureen's spiritual director) by nodding Their Heads toward him, and a light came from Blessed Mother's Heart onto Father Kenney.

Jesus: "I am your Jesus, born Incarnate. My brothers and sisters, do not languish longer in disbelief, for this is the compromise Satan presents to you, to keep you from living the Message of Holy and Divine Love. Nor should you allow your hearts to give in to the temptation of discouragement and fear. Trust in Me—trust in My Mercy. Await with joyful hope the coming victory of Our United Hearts."

"I have come to bring peace to hearts—hearts that will trust in My Mercy. My Divine Mercy is from age to age and from horizon to horizon upon the <u>repentant</u> heart. My Mercy falls upon all mankind, not out of deservedness, but out of each one's need."

"Once again I remind you that those who love Me—trust in Me. To trust in Me is to trust in the attribute of My Mercy. It is the unrepentant whose hearts I have come to change. These are the ones who do not look into their own hearts. They do not try to earn their salvation through love. This is why the world is torn asunder with every kind of sin. The fruit of these sins is war. Because so little value is placed upon human life, the sins today far outweigh the sins of Sodom and Gomorrah."

"This is why the Message and the Mission here of Holy and Divine Love far exceed any in attempting to form hearts in love. This is why the messages lay bare Satan—his snares and his tactics. Do not be surprised at the inroads Satan has made where he is exposed, or the types of sins which are now coming to light. This could not remain under the cover of darkness longer. While it is bringing down those in high places, even within the Church, it is necessary in order that the festering sore be healed. Many consciences now will be stripped of their compromise. Just as the mission here is the salvation of souls, it must be so in My Church, as well. Reputation and money cannot be first. All must be surrendered to Me."

"I tell you the greatest threat to mankind today is not terrorism, certain infamous and elusive leaders or even nuclear weapons. The greatest threat is the evil hidden in hearts that would exceed any lengths to obtain its end. I tell you there is an evil alliance forming in certain hearts which will come to light soon. This is not a war over territories or boundaries, but a war between good and evil."

"The Mission here—though ecumenical—will continue as a strong link to orthodoxy and tradition. It will become even stronger and sought out as a spiritual refuge amidst blight. The boundaries of this Mission will expand, both in hearts and in the world. The enemy's tongue will be tied. He will be seen to trip over his own tail. He will be seen to be like a lion without teeth or claws—harmless in the face of the good My Mission will accomplish."

"The Rosary of the Unborn will become the weapon of choice, both in Heaven and on earth in the war against abortion—so prepare for this. Take up your arms, children of God. Prepare! Stalemates which have affected My Mission until now will be resolved. Projects will continue and begin anew. Those who defend and assist this Mission, I will defend and assist. Those who make themselves your adversaries are My adversaries, as well. Today We are blessing you with the Blessing of Our United Hearts."

October 7, 2002

St. Thomas Aquinas comes. He bows before the tabernacle and says: "Praise be to Jesus."

"The Holy Mother has sent me to talk to you about the Rosary. Some people—even Church leaders—make light of it, you know. But the power of the Rosary has not changed over the centuries. If more would pray it, abortion would be recognized for what it is. The acceptance of abortion by any country's leaders places the country in jeopardy; for this sin alone brings about wars, natural disasters, political confusion and economic collapse."

"Devotion to the Holy Rosary places the soul under the Blessed Mother's protection—certainly a place anyone should seek to be during these times. Carrying the rosary with you is a sign to Satan that you belong to Mary."

"Meditation upon the mysteries of the Rosary brings the soul closer to Jesus, and leads him away from sin. The Rosary is a decisive weapon against Satan's kingdom in this world."

"Once the soul begins daily recitation of the Rosary, the Blessed Mother pursues him—seeking his sanctity and deeper commitment to prayer."

"Make this known."

MESSAGES FROM THE ETERNAL FATHER

October 4, 2000

"I am Lord of the morning and Keeper of the night. I fix the sun, the moon, and the stars in their place. I spill the rain from Heaven to nourish the earth. I press the chill against your cheek when you arise. Unnumbered are the miracles of My creation. I am the Eternal Father, Patriarch of all generations. I Am Who Am."

"Thus shall you remember Me and depend upon Me – trusting all the while in My Divine Provision which falls upon all mankind as dew upon the tender grass. As the world was created by a perfect Hand, learn to look for My perfection in every present moment. The tapestry I weave for each soul is unprecedented, the opportunities of grace abundant and irreproachable. I draw you into the secret-most Chambers of My Son's Eternal Heart."

October 6, 2000

"I am the Eternal Father, Creator of the Universe. It is I Who command the seasons. It is I Who call life from the earth in the spring. I Who bring forth the young and succulent new life. It is I Who renew the earth, and bring the soft showers to wash away the dormant. I am in the strong wind that forces the clouds past the sun and lifts the dry leaves off of tender new plants."

"I am in the summer, heating the air with My loving Breath so that all of nature bears fruit in due season."

"It is I, the Eternal Father, Who in the chill autumn night paints every leaf of all My trees in a perfect pattern so that when you arise you can marvel at My handiwork."

"I am Lord over all the harvest, the grains of the fields, the fruits and vegetables. It is I Who bear them forth – the plenty of My bounty."

"In the winter, once again, I give earth Her rest. I chill the air and fill the sky with snowflakes, each one My Own design. A hush falls over earth and for a moment My Benevolent Heart can be felt to beat as My children await the birth of My Only Begotten Son."

"On which season do I show My greatest favor? On all, just as My plan for each soul is individual and perfect in My Divine Will. I order all things mightily."

HOW DO I PRAY THE ROSARY?

The Rosary has been prayed since the thirteenth century. While meditating on the life of Jesus, one recites the prayers that bring one closer to Him and to His Mother, Mary.

During the Rosary, we say the Glory Be as *"All Glory Be…"* and also pray *"Jesus, Protect and Save the Unborn"* after each mystery. *These are at Our Lady's request.*

1. **Opening Prayers**

- *Begin by raising your rosary to heaven and saying:*

Celestial Queen, with this rosary, we bind all sinners and all nations to your Immaculate Heart.

- *Then make the **Sign of the Cross**:*

   In the name of the Father, and of the Son and of the Holy Spirit. Amen.

- *Then pray the following prayers:*

   ### Prayer for the Conversion of Hearts

   Heavenly Father, during this time of world crisis, let all souls find their peace and security in Your Divine Will. Give each soul the grace to understand that Your Will is Holy Love in the present moment.

   Benevolent Father, illuminate each conscience to see the ways that he is not living in Your Will. Grant the world the grace to change and the time in which to do it. Amen.
   (Our Lady gave this prayer to the visionary right after the 9/11 terrorist attack on New York.)

   ### Prayer to Recite with the Rosary of the Unborn

   Divine Infant Jesus, as we pray this rosary, we ask you to remove from the heart of the world the desire to commit the sin of abortion. Remove the veil of deceit Satan has placed over hearts which portrays promiscuity as a freedom, and reveal it for what it is—slavery to sin.

Place over the heart of the world a renewed respect for life at the moment of conception. Amen.
   (Our Lady August 27, 2005)

- *Then recite the **Apostles' Creed**:*

I believe in God, the Father Almighty, Creator of Heaven and earth; and in Jesus Christ, His only Son Our Lord, Who was conceived by the Holy Spirit, born of the Virgin Mary, suffered under Pontius Pilate, was crucified, died, and was buried. He descended into Hell; the third day He rose again from the dead; He ascended into Heaven, and sitteth at the right hand of God, the Father almighty; from thence He shall come to judge the living and the dead. I believe in the Holy Sprit, the holy Catholic Church, the communion of saints, the forgiveness of sins, the resurrection of the body and life everlasting. Amen.

- *Next pray one **"Our Father"** (for the intentions of the Holy Father); three **"Hail Mary's"** (for the virtues of Faith, Hope and Charity); and then one **"All Glory Be:"***

Our Father, Who art in heaven, Hallowed be Thy Name. Thy Kingdom come. Thy Will be done, on earth as it is in Heaven. Give us this day our daily bread. And forgive us our trespasses, as we forgive those who trespass against us. And lead us not into temptation, but deliver us from evil. Amen.

Hail Mary, full of grace, the Lord is with thee; Blessed art thou among women, and blessed is the fruit of thy womb, Jesus. Holy Mary, Mother of God, pray for us sinners, now and at the hour of death. Amen.

All Glory Be to the Father, and to the Son, and to the Holy Spirit. As it was in the beginning, is now, and ever shall be, world without end. Amen.

2. **The Mysteries of the Rosary**

   (**Note:** Pope John Paul II proposed the following schedule for those praying a 5-decade Rosary: *Joyful* on Monday and Saturday; *Luminous* on Thursday; *Sorrowful* on Tuesday and Friday; and G*lorious* on Wednesday and Sunday.)

   - *After <u>each Mystery</u>, recite the following prayers while meditating on the Mystery:*

Our Father...Ten Hail Mary's...All Glory Be...the Fatima Ejaculation... and the Unborn Ejaculation...

Fatima Ejaculation

O my Jesus, forgive us our sins, save us from the fires of hell, lead all souls to heaven, especially those who are most in need of Thy mercy.

Unborn Ejaculation

Jesus, Protect and Save the Unborn!

3. **Prayers After the Rosary**

Hail, Holy Queen, Mother of Mercy! Our life, our sweetness and our hope! To Thee do we cry, poor banished children of Eve; to Thee do we send up our sighs, mourning and weeping in this valley of tears. Turn, then, most Gracious Advocate, Thine Eyes of mercy toward us, and after this our exile, show unto us the blessed Fruit of Thy Womb, Jesus. O clement, O loving, O sweet Virgin Mary.

V. Pray for us, O Holy Mother of God.

R. That we may be made worthy of the promises of Christ.

Let us pray. O God, whose only begotten Son, by His life, death and resurrection, has purchased for us the rewards of eternal life. Grant, we beseech Thee, that meditating upon these Mysteries in the most Holy Rosary of the Blessed Virgin Mary, we may imitate what they contain, and obtain what they promise through the same Christ, Our Lord, Amen.

4. **Prayers for the Holy Father**

- *Recite the following prayers for the intentions and well-being of Our Holy Father:*

    Our Father... Hail Mary... All Glory Be...

- *Make the **Sign of the Cross**:*

    In the Name of the Father, and of the Son and of the Holy Spirit. Amen.

PRO-LIFE MEDITATIONS ON THE MYSTERIES OF THE ROSARY
By Fr. Frank Pavone, *Priests for Life*

Joyful Mysteries

1. <u>The Annunciation</u>
Mary is troubled by the angel's greeting, yet rejoices to do God's will. Let us pray that those who are troubled by their pregnancy may have the grace to trust in God's will.

2. <u>The Visitation</u>
John the Baptist leapt for joy in his mother's womb. We pray that people may realize that abortion is not about children who "might" come into the world, but is about children who are already in the world, living and growing in the womb, and are scheduled to be killed.

3. <u>The Nativity</u>
God Himself was born as a child. The greatness of a person does not depend on size, for the newborn King is very small. Let us pray for an end to prejudice against the tiny babies threatened by abortion.

4. <u>The Presentation</u>
The Child is presented in the Temple because the Child belongs to God. Children are not the property of their parents, nor of the government. They - and we - belong to God Himself.

5. The Finding of Jesus in the Temple
The boy Jesus was filled with wisdom, because He is God. Let us pray that all people may see the wisdom of His teachings about the dignity of life, and may understand that this teaching is not an opinion, but the truth.

Luminous Mysteries

1. Christ is Baptized in the Jordan
When Jesus is baptized, the Father's voice is heard: "This is my beloved Son." All are called to become adopted sons and daughters of God through baptism. We pray that children in the womb may be protected, so that they may be born and welcomed into the Christian community by baptism.

2. Christ is made known at the Wedding of Cana
Jesus revealed His glory by the miracle at Cana. The new couple was blessed not only with wine, but with faith in Christ. Let us pray for strong marriages, rooted in the Lord, and open to the gift of new life.

3. Christ proclaims the Kingdom and Calls All to Conversion
"Repent and believe the Good News." Let us pray that these first words of Jesus' public ministry may be heard by all who have committed abortion. May they know that the Lord calls them to conversion, and may they experience life-giving repentance.

4. The Transfiguration
Christ is transformed on the mountain, and the disciples see His glory. May the eyes of all people be transformed, that they may see each and every human life as a reflection of the glory of God Himself.

5. Jesus gives us the Eucharist
"This is My Body, given up for you." The Eucharist teaches us how to live and how to love. Let us pray that parents who sacrifice the babies for the sake of themselves may learn instead to put themselves aside for the sake of their babies.

Sorrowful Mysteries

1. The Agony in the Garden
Let us pray for mothers and fathers who are in agony because they are tempted to abort a child. May they be given the good news that there are alternatives, and may they make use of the help that is available.

2. The Scourging
As Christ's flesh was torn by the instruments of those who scourged Him, so the bodies of babies in the womb are torn by the instruments of the abortionists. Let us pray that abortionists may repent of these acts of child-killing.

3. The Crowning With Thorns
Jesus suffered the pain of thorns in His head, and did so silently. We pray for the mothers and fathers of aborted

children. So many of them suffer deep grief and regret over a choice they can never reverse. So many suffer in silence, because others tell them it's no big deal.

4.   The Carrying of the Cross
Jesus was not condemned by the power of wicked people. He was condemned because of the silence of good people. Silence always helps the oppressor, never the victim. Let us pray that we may never be silent about abortion, but rather will clearly speak up to save babies from death.

5.   The Crucifixion
As we ponder the death of Christ, let us remember the many women who have died from so-called "safe, legal" abortions. Let us ask forgiveness and mercy for them. May their memory save other women from making this tragic mistake.

Glorious Mysteries

1.   The Resurrection
Christ is Risen! By his Resurrection, He has destroyed the power of death, and therefore the power of abortion. The outcome of the battle for Life has already been decided: Life is victorious! Let us pray that all pro-lifers will spread this victory to every segment of our society.

2.   The Ascension
By ascending to the Father's throne, Christ takes our human nature, given to us in the womb, to the heights of

heaven. He shows us that human beings are made to be raised to heaven, not thrown in the garbage. Let us pray that the world may learn this truth and reject abortion.

3. The Descent of the Holy Spirit

The Holy Spirit is the Advocate: He pleads our cause, for we cannot save ourselves. We pray that He will make us advocates for the babies, who cannot speak or write or vote or protest or even pray.

4. The Assumption

The Blessed Virgin Mary was taken body and soul into heaven because she is the Mother of God. Mother and child are united. The Assumption reminds us that they belong together. We pray that society will see that it cannot love women while killing their children, and cannot save children without helping their mothers. We pray that people will be touched by the pro-life question, "Why can't we love them both?"

5. The Coronation

Mary is the Queen of the Universe. The Church teaches that she is the greatest creature, second only to God Himself. The Church defends the dignity of women. We pray that people will understand that to be pro-life means to be pro-woman, and that to be pro-woman demands that we be pro-life.

Permission has been granted for duplication and distribution of Meditations by Priests for Life.

Archangel Gabriel Enterprises Inc.
37137 Butternut Ridge Road   North Ridgeville, OH 44039
Phone: 440-327-4532
E-mail customerservice@rosaryoftheunborn.com
To order online: www.RosaryOfThe Unborn.com